Balancing the Elements

Palewell Press

Balancing the Elements

Poems by Helen Boyles

Balancing the Elements

First edition 2021 from Palewell Press,
www.palewellpress.co.uk

Printed and bound in the UK

ISBN 978-1-911587-51-4

All Rights Reserved. Copyright © 2021 Helen Boyles. No part of this publication may be reproduced or transmitted in any form or by any means, without permission in writing from the author. The right of Helen Boyles to be identified as the author of this work has been asserted by her in accordance with the Copyright, Designs and Patents Act 1988

The cover design is Copyright © 2021 Camilla Reeve
The front-cover image of a balancing rock at Epworth, Harare, Zimbabwe is Copyright © 2021
https://www.shutterstock.com/g/KITAMU
The photo of Helen Boyles is Copyright © 2021 Helen Boyles

A CIP catalogue record for this title is available from the British Library.

Dedication

I dedicate this collection to all members of my family for whom poetry has been a door out of the dark in challenging times.

Acknowledgements

- The poem 'Ash' received a Highly Commended nomination in the 2019 Edward Cawston Thomas Prize–the judge being ex-laureate Andrew Motion–and was included in a volume: 'A Nest of Singing Birds' published in the same year by the Edward Thomas Fellowship.
- 'The White Lands and The Black' was published in *Moor Poets IV* of contemporary poetry, Moor Poets, 2018.
- 'Hidden' was published in the Winter 2015 and 'Green Man' in the Summer 2019 editions of *Dawntreader, Indigo Dreams Publishing.*
- A recording of 'Hidden Springs' was accepted for the Poetry Society Archives in 2020.
- 'A Study in Blue and White' was displayed in a collaborative art/poetry exhibition in Birdwood House, Totnes, November 2019.
- 'Fossil Birds', 'The Nightingale', 'War-Song' and 'Troika!' were displayed in a collaborative art/ poetry exhibition in TAAG in Teignmouth, 2016 and 2018.

Contents

FOREWORD	1
WATER	3
Hidden Springs	4
Study in Blue and White	6
Odyssey	7
Seal Shadow	8
Asking forgiveness of the Albatross	10
The Last Hunter	12
AIR AND SPACE	15
Indian Moon	16
An Emptying	18
Night Shore	19
Kielder	20
Prisoner	21
ROCK AND FIRE	23
Glowworms, Kakahi	24
Hidden	26
Ash	28
Compostela	30
Riding to the Commandment Stone	32
Geothermal	34
Fossil Birds	35
FORESTS AND TREES	37
Green Man	38
The Nightingale	39

The Chestnuts	40
Waldwanderung	41
Amazon	42
BALANCING	43
Song of the Bones	44
Swan's Wing Burial	46
Briseis	48
I, Phillipus	50
Yeavering Bell	52
The White Lands and the Black	54
Winter's Mouth	56
War-Song	57
Breton	58
Sky-dancer above Haworth	60
The Medical Tent	62
The Voices of Aberfan	64
Old Dog	65
Spaces	66
Keeping Steady	68
'The Man on the Wall': a view from the other side	70
Handstander	72
Troika!	73
The Voices	74
Balancing	76
The Sea	78
Helen Boyles - Biography	81

FOREWORD

Balancing the Elements grew out of reflection on movements in nature and our human connection with those movements. The first part of the collection celebrates nature's variety and our intimacy with it while registering its vulnerability. Poems are framed in the elements and natural components of Water, Sky, Rock and Wood around which our lives are sometimes precariously balanced. The latter part of the collection focuses more closely on human experience with additional reflections on human movements within physical space and historical time. Within this broader context, the whole acknowledges a natural and human independency which we ignore at the risk of destabilising the balance essential to survival.

Helen Boyles

WATER

Hidden Springs

The day gapes bright again,
throat taut for rain and seep of dew,
leaves glossed already with sun
lifting shine of gold and green.
Some edges are still sharp,
some shrubs on the edge of wilt.
Birds pant open-beaked,
seek glint of moisture in the bowls
we've placed around.

But stop and listen close
and we can hear the shrivelled hum
of hidden springs.
We must creep back down the old path,
nose out the sources that sleep
deep in the wood.

We stumbled on them there the other day,
the springs, their beds carved out and sealed
with clay, roofed with mossed slate,
their secret doors almost invisible –
found Bat Well Spring where black serrated wings
still fray the shift of day to night.

The water lies there like a crystal glass
reflecting our forgotten face,
the source that fed the farms and homes,
from which our lives and thoughts
come bubbling up.
It is a living tongue, a birthing song
we must replenish and recall,
draw on its cool to slake our thirst,
remember where we rise and thrive,
where we can fall.

Study in Blue and White

A response to an abstract art work by Maggie Anne-Smith.

In ocean, water sinks
to its own silences,
to a sleep of indigo flicked
with the luminous tremor
of minute passages
a world beneath the speed
and spin of surfaces.

Ocean holds its knowledge,
holds its own.
Now and then its curtained fall
is nudged by deeper shadows
and another light,
by a questing cycle of whales
rising from the deepest caves,
opening the spaces outside
and within.

Vast and barnacled, in their slow time
they travel continents.
Now, in shaping eye of pen
or brush they heave and swell
to ice floes at the climate's edge,
as we gaze within the globe,
the artist's page, swim into view
and out again,
fracture and dissolve
to distances.

Odyssey

Looping the rhythms of her span
water travels through her blood,
pulls her to the birthing beds
to empty treasure, float
a bloom of pearls
over the rippling flats.
Pearled seeds swell to darkened pupils,
split to fry, sliver to smelts
that thread the river's travelling.

Through seasons she wears the rainbow
of the roaming light reflecting stone
and sky. Slow pulse is knitted
to the river's artery that opens
to the ocean's glittering,
call of the moon-drawn tides.

She twists through knots of danger,
journey shadowed by the mesh and hook
of predator until the final wall
of ribboned colour she must fail
or crest in slice and flash of scale,
curve of tail, must peak and sink
to the cradle pool of origins,
rush stilled to purpose, calm eye
globing life and death:
sacrificial gift to her continuing.

Seal Shadow

We had to ride the waves
rolling to surf on easterlies that afternoon,
let it take us, loose-limbed from the routine day
to empty us in water's lift and pull,
frayed edge of salt air on the tongue,
antiseptic sting on skin.

The water grows opaque and strange as we swim
farther out, our floating, star-shaped bodies
newly luminous.

Smooth weight, cool curve beneath our legs,
a rounding, curling, silken pressure
sliding by us –
gone.
sleek stroke on belly, thigh, a gentle buffeting
then gone.

Now, a twist of shadow and a mottled
silver gleam of head breaks surface,
rises up and holds our startled gaze
in whiskered curiosity -
there, and there again emerges,
and with nostril flare and liquid eye
another bullet-dark head periscopes.

They observe as if remembering,
as if greeting after absences.
We speak, they listen; in our raised heads
we hold a shared space, see ourselves
mirrored in dark pools of folk memory
metamorphosed into Selkie
joined in yearning
for the freedom of this element.

Quick swerve and deep dive
follows us with breathing grunts and sighs
beneath our flexing feet, voice, limbs
melding in a braid of breath and current
out beyond the marker buoys

till watching cliffs summon us back,
sea shrinks to shore and we return
to struggle over stones on land-feet,
shake off spray and scent,
draw on human skin and fibre coats
as our seal shadow slips away, melts
to the wide bay,
strands us on a dry shore
bruised by light.

Asking forgiveness of the Albatross

We perch this morning on the bright shore
for a first encounter with age-old denizens
of earth and myth.
Seasoned skipper, sea and bird-wise,
great respecter of the Queen
and partnership of commonwealth,
meets and greets then cuts a clean path out,
out into the Bay's wide glittering.
Beyond, a stride of peaks climb white
against sky's abalone,
below, a silver scroll of mist, and now, from there,
glide giants on great wings
growing towards us,
another kingdom opening.

Angels carved in ebony and ivory
they beat their slow flight through a dance
of fairy petrel playing air and spume
to congregate and claim the rich gift
trailing from the stern,
accept our peace offering.

Their heraldic heads are heavy
with the knowledge of other lands
and distances, the thousands of sea miles
travelled in their parenting.
We feel humbled that they condescend to visit us.
This is a new world; we have learned
from the errors of the old, or so we like to think,
distance ourselves from the predations
of the hunting, whaling days.

So we welcome, feed the Albatross,
and it speeds us through the sunlit foam,
wide wings steadying our way.

The Last Hunter

A response to documentary film: The last Igloo.

The morning window
widens to space and a white light,
strikes his waking with its silences.
He leaves the sleeping house,
feels the crisp earth answer his tread,
sees ahead the tethered huskies rouse, stretch
at his summons and the runners' scrape.

He trusts their knowledge of the ice,
the way they fan when it is thin,
bunch when sound.
He has this – his voice, the clamour of the dogs,
paws speeding the track,
the sharpened frost, the sighing sweep
of wilderness.
He has his whittled stick, his knife,
his measuring eye and hand
to pierce and carve out breathing holes,
suspend the water net for fish or seal,
has patience, and for now, has time
to find the right snow, test its density,
cut blocks to stack and mould
into a shelter dome secure from storm.

He trusts to earth's provision,
the dogs wait too for his.
But something else will overtake
their time. 'Our world is shrinking', he says.
'Once I could travel anywhere across
the frozen space. Now sea laps
where we ran the sledge.

Out in the bright and singing emptiness
colours flash from ice to sky,
from blue to gold to green,
seep from minerals and lichens,
deepen in the waters of the lake.
They are the colours at creation's birth
and finishing.

He nurses the last warmth of his lantern
as the one lit cave slowly revolves, recedes,
floats out on water, dark,
a solitary star.

AIR AND SPACE

Indian Moon

Snow-filled bowl of winter moon
holds its vigil through the long dark,
whitens plain and wood,
spreads to the huddled red of hearth
in Full Snow Moon.
Howl of hungry wolves
in deep woods on the hill
throws a snare around
the human gathering
in Full Wolf Moon.

Cool, but kinder moon
of winter's edge
swims from trees,
sheds the shadow
of the crow's wing,
last cry echoing,
in Crow Moon.

Moon empties glitter on the lake,
marks the seep of spring melt
underneath the snow's ridge,
frosts it over with night's breath
in Crust Moon,
watches worm-threads in the sliding ground
in Worm Moon,

rounds to the frugal plate of Lenten Fast
at settlers' Eastertide
in Lenten Moon,
answers the warmth of flowers' blush
in April's Pink Moon,
blooms in the fragrance of the short warm night
in Flower Moon
draws out the ruby light and scent of summer fruit
in Strawberry Moon or Rose.

Moon crowns the time of sprouting velvet
in the young Buck's Moon,
mirrors shoals of sturgeon
rising on the flood
in Sturgeon Moon,
sinks its silver in the gold of autumn corn
in Harvest Moon
opens up the shorn steppes
to the eye of predator
in Hunter's Moon.

Beneath Moon's rise and pull,
land turns through the year
slowly, but certainly,
lifts water,
sinks the seed,
wakes or soothes the beast,
drives the rhythms
of the hunter,
farmer,
gatherer.

An Emptying

Ted Hughes referred to the annual migratory return of hirondines as a sign that the world was still turning.

Is the world still turning to and from the sun
from sleep to day on its diurnal tilt,
but always tipping back to spring –
Is it still turning?
It is May and there are no swallows,
no racing shapes above us
scissoring the sky.
Maybe the world has stiffened on its axis,
frozen our winged messengers.
And thieves wait at the gates of their escape,
smothering their dance in mists of net.

Their sky-shapes are the arrows of our faith
speeding out and back again
to the heart's home. They centre us.
Through summer we would see them
dip to the water's brim, scoop up the light,
see them flicker in a corner of the eye
the reds and blues of courting dress,
hear them gossip on the wires and eaves.
Now the eye reflects the sky's blank, mirrors
an emptying,
and the voiceless spaces of the dawn and evening
are a kind of death.

Night Shore

The stars which prick this dark
are the voices
of birds
which fan in glinting shoals
along the night shore.
They pulse and recede
as we pass by,
shine
in sudden clusterings.
We brush the edge
of other deepnesses
thronged
with quick feet, bright eyes
invisible to us,
the shimmer, lilt
and falling
of their loosened threnody
the shivering
of light
beyond, above
the spaces we have lost.

Kielder

Last lights thin and melt behind us
as we motor into space that slowly
spreads to forest deepening to dark
along the coils of an empty road.
We tunnel though strangeness, silence,
to a final opening.
Stands of black trees wait, watch
where great eyes, lapped in metal
within shuttered frames
rear, slowly revolve.
They are looking at something else
outside our pinched horizons:
another dark, lights from otherwhere
shimmering their veils across the black.

Clambering onto the scaffolding
we gaze up through the giant lens of gods,
see the shining of our origins
and destinies in scatterings of particles,
a cosmic circumvolve.
See we are here, we are there,
we have been, will be something other
than we know, swelling and dying
through infinities of memory.

Around us the forest is prowling with shapes
flung up in constellations.
Wolves will be stalking here, they say,
before too long.
The pad of their night hunt sounds in our blood.
With them we raise our heads, float
outside ourselves,
hail from some drowned source
the clear ring of the stars.

Prisoner

In costume drawn to startle predators
it curled into a secret cavity
to slowly push through skins of change
and stiffen to another form.
Through the cycling dial of the sun
outside, unseen, it crafted an anatomy
that casked a fold of silks. In time,
blood pricked the membrane net
that itched to break to light and flight,
burst to a trembling spread of lime and rose
above the shine of latticed gaze:
gift for the sky, the leaf, the stem.

But through its patient metamorphosis
our hasty building pace
had bricked the cradle mouth.
One day it was uncovered
by dismantling hands, perfect
but dead, soft as dust in its blind cell,
globed eyes reflecting back
the darkness, no air to stir
and free its untried wings.

ROCK AND FIRE

Glowworms, Kakahi

You can't see them from here, but they are there,
and he pointed down the tunnel
of the abandoned railway cutting
at the end of a forgotten track.
No, believe me, they're there in their thousands-
Go and see.
So I returned along the path
between the sheared rock-face
shaggy with fern, and in its secret dark
it was as if the sky had slipped
and emptied all its stars into that one space,
catching, as they fell, on leaves and fronds,
snagging on jagged edges and in cracks
where they chinked their brilliance.
When you looked up from below
they jewelled the roof of caves and crevices.

I knew the stars were hungry larvae
snaring prey with sticky, iridescent threads,
but, for us, they were a shining festival.
You have to stand and face them, he had said.
If you look at them obliquely they will fade:
turn aside, they disappear.
And so I faced them and was filled
with wonderment. As I gazed, more
and yet more opened their eyes to mine
till I was circled in their shimmering.

Yes, when I saw, I could accept the miracle,
but as the lights went out one by one
when I returned and left them at my back
and the path shrunk to distance,
it was as though they'd never been.

Hidden

This is where the treasure is,
underneath our feet
and beyond that.
It sleeps
and slowly turns
in the half light
to quiet unfolding of our origins
in earth time,
sea time,
time beyond memory.
Beauty blooms
in the ink dark of the sea,
inscribes in messages
the folded page of rock.
We tramp, race,
chatter,
smother the buried levels
with ephemera,
distracted with anxieties
and busyness.
For now
I perch on 400 million years
of crushed bone
scanning the waves,
adjusting artificial sights
to frame the rounding back,
quick slice of fin,
the wide-winged bird
plunging to hidden shoals.
Just for a moment
here, there
and here again

I see its gleam, its poise,
its shining edge.
It rolls and glides in worlds
beyond our knowing
luckily
but we can float the mind
out on its surface,
catch its light,
dream,
feel the pulse of its passing.

Ash

Without knowing the cause, in 1793, Hampshire clergyman Gilbert White recorded in his diary the destructive impacts on Britain of a massive volcanic eruption in Iceland felt over two winters.

His diary registered the struggling light,
the smothered air, the failure
of his orchard buds again that spring.
In his garden he observed bees
shrivelled in their brittle beds,
first shoots limp in tended plots,
heard from the fields lambs cry
in the frost, spades strike the iron
of the soil's crust.

Hope stumbling with wasted crops,
lives fell in dim interiors.
He could only murmur pious comforts
to the hopeless, close their eyes for them.

Far from his knowing, out across the northern waves,
a mountain fractured, burst, poured out
its molten energy, for two years
billowed its pall across the sea and sun.
He breathed a bitterness, tasted ash on his tongue.

He remarked how hirondines that other years
had gossiped, jostled in the eaves
had not appeared this time.
But one day, shrunk in warmer corners of his barn
he found a hare, a passage bird or two,
a trembling hind.
He caught her wild eye, but did not
startle her away.

All this he noted in his journal
as dark fires smouldered in another land.
He puzzled to connect the signs, detect
the causal force: God's hand? Some message,
punishment? For what?
He could not presume to understand.

Compostela

Lit porch of welcome in a strange town,
sleep in the stripped white of a convent room.
Morning, and a stone trudge up steps
to the great door opening to walls humming
with litany. Blessing in mixed tongues
spilt on our flagged descent to the *Via*
forged by Romans for control and trade,
printed by the faithful unshod
measuring the way in hope and weariness,
marking leagues in wood and rock.

We press the strata of their buried lives,
feel through our soles the earth's slow build
and settling, tune to the low hiss of change,
the seep of minerals that feed the springs,
mould to the sand-sift of the forest *sentier*,
the limestone *causse,* volcanic crust,
hold our ground and nerve above the plunge
of wooded gorge.

Muscles are stretched and substance thinned
to melting passages through sun, rain, mist
as we expand, contract to toiling specks,
to pulses in the galaxy, are lost, found,
refashioned, know our beginnings, end,
know ourselves fired in the potter's kiln,
crumbled from sky to earth dust,
star to bone.

Ribs of *la concha*, paths fan to the crown
of the Cathedral's worked stone, grand
swing of the *fumeiro*, sounding bell,
recede on a thinning, shining thread
beyond to the space of Finisterre:
the final opening:
Begin again.

Riding to the Commandment Stone

Reared on moor, half bristling bent,
half wet, your feet know the ground,
know to skirt the scoops and shallows,
not to risk the stumble and the skid of hoof
on puddled peat.
You scent the sluice of rain in moss,
slow seep of decay,
fresh shoots, the sun-warmed rock.

You let me steer but take the lead
along the sound path up the beacon
that had flared Armada's coming
centuries ago, now stand while I peer
at the Commandment Stone with *Shalt Not*s
newly etched from lichen creep.
You wait as I trace the words
that thunder silently
to the invisible.

We balance our weight on monuments,
carve them with creeds of faith and fear
to root our wanderings
but shadow-shift of cloud and wind and sun
blur boundaries and certainties,
strand us in space.

Horizons billow dark
then sun swims out to light the valley floor.
Your shod feet, twitching ear and eye
measure the nearer way from stable yard
uphill to moorland and the open heights,
back down across the forded stream
and home again.
Dismounting for the final lap,
and grounded, our feet move together
steadily, complete the simple cycle
of the known and sure.

Geothermal

We are dancing on the skin of the earth it seems,
flirting with water, heat and steam,
fashioning a wonderland from forces
hurtling through gorges, seeping from crevices,
bubbling up from vivid lesions in the polished rock.
Charmed by the bell-notes in trees overhanging caves
we twist and turn between the gaps and edges,
idly register the muffled voice beneath our feet
of something building, something disturbed.
Earth's erratic rhythms do not match
our neater measures; it sleeps fitfully
through all our busyness, the spaces
in our chattering.

Beyond our pleasure ground we choose
not to see the fissures widen,
do not attend too closely to the primal pressure-valve's
slow hiss of escaping energy.

Fossil Birds

Feathers brushed air,
gleamed colour in the sun's eye,
wings played the thermals,
hung on updrafts
in strange latitudes,
beaks pointed flight paths,
threw weird calls from trees
now crumbled to carbon,
compressed to stone.

They sleep there too now,
head tucked in a new birth,
sink their blues and greens
and purples in earth minerals,
wait across millennia
to be opened up to light again,
their delicate anatomy
unpicked by careful hands.

FORESTS AND TREES

Green Man

Churchyard's shadow priest and guardian,
old before the church's birth, 1283,
he spans a millennium,
knots histories in bark and root,
wraps generations with their tilted headstones
in a tortuous embrace.
He is nourished by a sunken city
of mycelia which web the secret dark,
swell his capillaries,
prick autumn litter with bright caps.
He bears gifts, his jewelled berry-crop
enticing eye and tongue, safe only
if you spit the bitter pip:
he can defend himself from enemies.

Christian and Pagan are interleaved
and folded in his corded book:
evergreen quill-tips score
the shredded parchment of the sky
with figures of eternity:
church bells toll in his bones.
He fosters faith and ritual,
is ringed with myth, and if
you want to know a future lover
you must circle his great girth
three times widdershins
before he ghosts an answer
that holds sure so long
as there is no one looking on.

The Nightingale

once threw its voices out across the peasant's tilled plot
from the forest edge,
looped the ramblings of wood-wanderers at dusk,
was spied by a farmer-poet in the low scrub of shared heath
where he saw its bright eye, trembling throat,
tried to transcribe its language on the page.
The Nightingale
duetted nightly with a cellist in a Surrey copse,
dwelt in riddles and romances, shape-shifted
into myth.

As time closes in on us, so the nightingale
shrinks back.
Now we unravel the ribbons of its song
and weave them in a glowing cage,
score its melody with human instruments
as haunting themes for ballads, melancholy films,
capture it in machine recordings,
casket it in poems, art's iconography.

We celebrate and try to hold it safe
while it wing-slips from our grasp
and, teasing ventriloquist,
echoes back our longing
as it vanishes, melts
into memory.

The Chestnuts

are allowed to grow old here
in their sweet, slow time.
They cycle the sun and rain of seasons
steadily, know the secrets of the earth,
draw deep on them to plump their crop
and burnish it.
They have shaped another beauty
in their calloused skin, contorted arms
and bulging girth:
a proud disfiguring.
Now autumn peels its rust to the floor,
leaves shed their late light.

A hare enters, moves across the quiet glade,
ears showing white, alert to threat.
Along the track are stationed two camions
where hunters prime their guns
for the October shoot.
They target the quick and free;
the hare must hide and run.
The trees,
weighted with age
and riches for our bowls
are safe.

Waldwanderung

The forest nets the city in its stirring screen,
wraps it in a history of hunting, folk-memory
of stories waymarked by the sudden flit of birds,
shadowed by the pad of predator,
pooled in the wary eye of grazing hinds.
As we step out on the *Fussweg*
we are watched, but do not know by what
or where.
A silence stalks our steps
but we are safe if we observe the rules:
we must not leave the path and try to forge
another way, nor pick the blooms that glow
in clearings, must not startle
the inhabitants we cannot see
but wait for us to go,
must not efface their tracks.

We are not the forest's masters,
though may think we are;
we can lose our bearings along forest rides
that lead us back where we began
or to a space we do not recognise
where all the signs are changed
and *Fledermäuse* flash black signatures
against the failing light.
We must shift and slow to older rhythms,
tune to different dialects
so are not left stranded
and bewildered on the edge of night
without a code we can translate,
without a compass that aligns us
to the forest's hidden, strange geometry.

Footnote: "Waldwanderung" - German for "Wandering in the woods"

Amazon

She folds rain curtains round herself,
lets it shine her skin, mist off her back
to steaming earth and dripping leaf.
She has been here for millennia,
first coiled in the roots of the great trees,
in swaying branches loosening her limbs,
from tangled tresses spilling fruit
and seed. In stippled sun-play
she takes on the camouflage of jaguar,
melts and glows with the chameleon,
moves to the lazy swing of sloth
drowsing in the dripping silence
between rains. She steadies
to the slow tread of the pachyderm,
panther-pads the shadows
to the drinking pool.

Now she is stalked by other predators
that envy her embrace of water,
leaf and stone, the rhythms
of her spreading and her gathering.
Their dull roar builds,
blades slash the sacramental light.
She folds the mysteries of praise
within herself, returns to curl again
in earth, thin to the flow of sap,
still her pulse in waiting
for another summoning.

BALANCING

Song of the Bones

So, perched on the mind's bridge
we are there, or were once,
clinging to the edge of things.
I can see us small on the shore
trawling the sea for nourishment,
piling ornamentally the carapace of feasts.
Until the seas rose, engulfed our marine gardens,
we scoured the sands, followed the herds,
used all of a kill to keep and clothe ourselves.
Light and dark swung their cycles
round us, guided us to work and sleep.

Then, the warming and silting of earth,
march of the trees, clearing of trees
and forest settlements.
We circled and announced our space
with ditches, bunds, rocks,
dug out and carved the flint to whittle blades
for weaponry, chinked their knapping
in the opened glades as smoke curled up.

Our hands were small, but thousands
over hours, days, years,
raised monuments, heaved histories.
Voices could call, feet tramp over distances,
scenting the earth for treasure
to exchange and store.

We turned with the solstice, in rough pillars
carved subtly angled apertures and passages
to catch and hold the sun.

Silent spill on stone, a faith distilled,
trembles against eclipse.

Swan's Wing Burial

In the late 1980s in Vedbaek, Denmark, a Mesolithic tomb was discovered which contained the bodies of a young mother and newborn baby enfolded in a swan's wing.

Neither had survived the journey through pain
and labour to the day; at its threshold slipped away,
but mother and newborn had been gathered,
laid together in the kind dark of the earth,
kernelled there in waiting for rebirth.

Curled round them, soft as morning cloud
was a swan's wing, just one white embrace
folding their sleep in a mute suspense.
The sky bent over them, mists wrapped them round,
held them secret in their slow time
till the opening to shock of spade and light.

It seemed the mother and her child had rocked a long way
on the swan's wing to this shore
to be uncovered finally by probing eyes and implements,
spread of bird wing shrunk to quills,
an offering for scientific scrutiny
of shredded fabric, bones and shells.

It felt a sacrilege to lift them
from their bed, to separate
and reassemble them.
Some shed a tear at this late point in time
to see their helplessness.

But they had long since taken flight,
been lifted to another light
upon the swan's great pinions,
strong and sure had climbed above the earth,
the water's skin, into the sky on its broad back
trailing their garments, far from generation's drag.
Now, wondering, they look back
at our huddled selves, here, small, puzzled,
staring down.

Briseis

Here on this shore the horizon
thins its spear of light to shine my robe, my gaze
to space where feet are winged to flight.
Who, what, where am I?
in this body planted on the sand,
arranged for pleasure on a soldier's bed?
Out there, burst from my carapace
and free?

The curtains of my infant sleep were parted
by my mother's hands, my father's face,
shadowed by their plans for me,
their needs and strategy.
And I was married well, had rank, security.
All that dissolved to Poseidon's catch,
and I, the spoils of war,
gift-wrapped in my brothers' blood,
became a hero's prize split open
by his triumph and his rage
and hollowed by his emptiness.

Who, what, where am I?
I am another thing to measure others' pride;
I will be moved across the board,
exchanged again, replaced.
For these seas at my life's edge stretch
to other lands and cities
to be torched and sacked,
lives bartered or laid waste.

If I had feet to run, a tongue to speak,
I could bellow the grief of this;
instead, in silence and in stillness
I must wait, wait for the tide to turn.
For I have a name;
it has a softness, but can twist
to a snake's hiss:
some will remember it.

I, Phillipus

Northern posting, sail-swept
to empire's edge, campaign shelter
whipped out to new distances,
sights held by the horizon's frown.
Earth contours flex in shift of climate,
slow shadow-dial of day to dusk.

As dawn turns its blade on the hill's crest,
dream-memory of courtyard fruit, sun-bruised,
fades from the tongue,
warmth shrinks from the skin.
These spaces, rain-dissolved, wind-scoured,
challenge the legions' might,
sharpening their elemental weapons
somehow diminish them.
They can't simply stand and brandish theirs;
the echoes ring back emptiness
and hidden threat.

They must plant a frontier,
must answer with the silences of stone,
sink and raise their purpose in pit and ditch,
in turf wall, high-stacked rock,
turrets stamping Roman miles
across the unmapped land,
carving an alphabet on wilderness.
But they cannot break the Whin Sill's back,
must mount and ride its sculpted, stern geology.

So how to pin identity to this indifference –
how inscribe authority? The Latin dialects,
the syllables of Syrian and African auxiliaries
are wind-dispersed, bedstraw and scabious
springing where they used to stand.
And all along its crumbled length at intervals
are signatures scoring the leagues:
I, Phillipus, Fifth Cohort, I, Florianus, Sixth Legion,
I, Germanicus, Seventh Cohort:
I built this:
I was here.

Yeavering Bell

We wade through mist that swum up
in the night, now hoods and mantles,
knits us in its dripping fleece.
Beyond are the hills we're making for,
invisible.
Ahead, another couple loom, emerge,
peering for the trig point promised by the map
as one by one the guiding signs
dissolve.
We try but fail to help, must take
our own soundings, trust to feet and sense
as did our ancestors.

And the curtain shreds and wavers
as we climb the flanks of Yeavering
through heather brush and peat,
peer on the heights for signatures
of those who long before us weathered worse,
knew rock and water's force,
the slow wheel of the light,
and learned to balance them,
used height and depth to carve security,
authority.
We trace the scoops and humps of ancient huts,
cloud-thatched, the tumbled lines
of a defended space.

Humbledon Hill, Broadstruthers, Yeavering Bell;
names echo the wind or quiet stuttered
with the bleat of goats,
ring through spreading walls of stone
or scour the air with battle cries.
We, faltering below, look up to see them,
see us striving to keep sights open,
trained on closer needs and distances,
stretching and combining to hold up the sky.

The White Lands and the Black

Stark on the summit,
dark on the bleached bent of the moor,
the gibbet is a rune
scored on the sky's blank.
Chains where a body hung
from its outstretched arm,
drip in the mist,
anchored foot rusts in the peat.
The angle of its one eye
holds the vastnesses,
funnels mind's imaginings
into the white land, the black,
the acid and the sand of heights and deeps,
lives lapped in earth and sky,
plans hatched in the secret shafts
of consciousness.

The crumbled Saxon cross beneath
may try to shame the memory,
cannot erase the signature
of violence and punishment, some half-
remembered tale of rivalry or bitterness,
a struggle and a smothered cry,
the fatal strike, abandoned corpse
and felon struggling to his sentence
through the slow clutch of the bog,
the long reach of the law.

We are warned: don't stumble here,
stray from the lighted path;
the place will spill you into emptiness,
fold you in its white breath,
tip you and tilt you,
float you on the curlew's keening
far to the sliding edge.

Winter's Mouth

Franklin's failed 1845 attempt to find the North-West passage.

So this is where it ended,
in a white silence
at the world's edge,
stricken arms of beached hull
piercing mist.
All is glittering, pristine,
but cruel as air stiffens
to a creaking cage
in stealthy hardening of frost
to crystal
sealing winter's mouth.

Space shrinks to a stage
furnished with books,
polished manners of the civilised,
fine dining at the captain's board.
The players wrapped their culture
round themselves,
tried to haul it out onto the cold shelf,
drag it behind them
in a wilderness they could not read
where senses, language
shrivelled to spent light.

Blood cannot seep into the melt
but congeals in the freeze
trapped in panes of ice
as signatures for seal-skinned,
wind-leathered hunters
decades on to struggle
to decipher, wonder at.

War-Song

Songs could be strung on memories of home,
worn under uniforms to the measure of the heart.
You could murmur their threads
when other noises swelled.
Ballad lyrics lifted voice, steps, in a plucky rhythm
slowed to the monotone trudge
of boots on long roads to the lines.

In the land that no-one owns, songs stutter
into dissonance; known syllables are spilt
from snapped threads or scored for strings
on barbed wire, tangled in their staves.
You had danced to courtship's patterns
in a country barn, another place of mind.
Here you dodge and dart and stumble
on the front where sets dissolve
and no one knows the moves,
shoulder the heavy dawns and darks
with stoic gaiety until a stealth attack
shocks limbs to spasm in a last dance
on the chasm's edge, flings life from sky
to mud.

Now colours sink into the petals
on memorials, songs are recast in the metal throats
of bugles, bells, where feet are stilled, heads bowed
to names intoned and graved in stone.

Breton

A response to the film: La Jeune Femme en Feu by Céline Sciamma.

Then she escapes from her closed home
into the dark, the dark trees,
sea's hush on shore below,
drawn by the jagged dance of flame
on wild hearth.
Eyes catch its light, spellbound;
she can warm her hands, face,
mind on it.

And there a gathering of women
in their caps and shawls, talking, laughing
in their dark, the dark trees.
And she walks among them, curious,
but unremarked, bathing in the shadows,
in the crackling and flickering,
drawn to the secret dark,
the dark trees.

Then a humming, building to an opened voice
catching the heart, speaking
beyond words the slow
swelling of the sea, the hidden
ringing of the rock,
wailing of wind-haunted space
all swept together through
one sound of striving, resting, birthing, dying,
holding, letting go,
eyes, mouth smiling as they sing
within and outside dialect
a spreading hive, sky-wide.

It brims her as she stands and gazes,
turns at last and moves away
back to the closed house,
skirts trailing flame.

Sky-dancer above Haworth

Grouse startle from our feet,
burst on the stillness their alarm
Go back! Go back! Go back!
Harsh against the brittle edge
of heather stems, calls rasp air,
graze the black burnt furrows
of the hunting field.
We intrude on their fastnesses:
eyes gleam in coverts warily.
But if we strip sense we can find
home, self, in the coarse roots,
dark earth, drifting sky.
Memories are laid down here,
sleep under skies and wind;
in night's spaces starlight
penetrates the secret script
of peat and rock.

Sudden! There! A dazzle lift and spread
of wings in bright clap
of triumphant flight
clean on the moor's height
soaring on thermals – hangs, falls
rises, turns, swoops down
and climbs again;
sky-dancing, pinion-powered,
persecuted bird
courts light.

Her rare spirit rises up
each time we crest that view,
ink-stippled pages flutter
from her outstretched arms.
Cloud flaps a cloak
around her spare frame
as, head into the wind,
she beats the miles with her bold stride,
eyes trained on shining levels
here and further off,
scorns discomfort, danger, wet,
half savage, hardy, free.

The Medical Tent

The light falls quietly in this screened space,
rests on bent heads, hands moving on the bench
among instruments, cycling the pestle
in its rhythmic grind.
Herbs hang from the canvas frame,
cast shade rubbed with scent of hill
and sun: Still Life beyond a waste of pain.
Flies patter their shadows on the screen,
thicken in places,
wait their opportunity.

Outside are bodies waiting to be mended,
groaning for the healing chill or sting
of poultice press, pain to be staunched,
flow stemmed and fractures sealed
or that severe relief for lives and limbs
beyond recovery.
War has brought them to this shore;
they are the lucky ones,
the rest claimed by the tide.

The bodies have minds that drift or tangle
in half-consciousness, the fever swells
and falls.
Safe memories, the moving eyes
and lips of faces known and loved
swim back, recede again, dissolve.
They may be held here for a space
then float away,
claimed by some other where.

So we injure, heal,
wound, then try to heal the damage,
wound, and struggle to repair ourselves,
wound.

The Voices of Aberfan

Through years' unburdening
the slag black mountain
inched up the window-panes
of classrooms at its base.
In daily chanting of times tables,
alphabets, it could be ignored,
shut behind blinds.
Warnings to industrial authorities
could be ignored.
But it stalked playground games
with its dark watch,
muffled the treble flights
of skipping rhymes,
mounted in corners of the mind.

Its voice came out eventually
as pressure shifted its slow sleep.
First, a trickle hush of ash
in its blind core,
a struggling breath.
Then as balance edged
to spill, a creaking, faint complaint
grew to grumble,
thickened to a low growl,
swelled.

'I felt it roar', she said, 'build and build
to thunder. Break.

And then
the most horrible silence I have ever heard.'

Old Dog

As sight has clouded, hearing dulled,
your sense perimeters have narrowed
to a nose that trawls the kitchen floor
and truffles garden space
for buried smells and scraps,
burrows in wayside weeds for signatures.
From puppyhood agility, movement
has stiffened to arthritic pottering
punctured by awkward scrabbling
inside and out, up and down steps.

But you can't mourn those bright-eyed,
happy-panting days of spring and bounce,
sigh at images of your ungrizzled self,
the gleam and gloss of youth,
slow seeping of its energy.
This – here, now, is all you know
and need.

You cannot regret, cannot anticipate,
just bend your dimmed eyes
on the one known face,
the hands, the feet that serve.
We, slung across wider spaces,
trapped between horizons, are slowed
and burdened by memory,
feel our bones.

Spaces

Restive in a closed space
each day he strode his steady energy
past our window, strong forward gaze,
calm authority of naval leadership
from other days.

Happier indoors, she always stayed
behind; she kept her space, he his,
though they rode the distance, smoothed
the differences with tenderness.
Sometimes, rarely, out together,
we would see them hand in hand,
his pace modified to hers,
her smile tucked to his.

Mostly she stayed still,
wrapped the known space round herself,
burrowed down and curtained it
more closely as time stretched
till shade by shade it sunk her
to a deeper place beyond the lift
of hands or face to kinder light.

Through trudging days his space
shrunk to hers, lapped its edge
protectively. He tried
to navigate that mist with her
which blurred her features, smothered
her articulate identity, tried to keep
his hand in her clasp as the tide withdrew.

Sometimes now we see them walk slowly
past our window, together
but apart, he, with eyes turned
her way, easing her journey down
with gifts her lonely child demands:
a ribbon, cake, bright fruit,
a green umbrella held carefully above her
on a dry day.

Keeping Steady

I watch the precise movements
of your practical, small hands
tending to our needs and comforts,
framing the business of the day.
Your mind is ordered into rooms
where tasks are ranged on shelves,
removed in turn,
renewed at intervals.
Memories are tied in ribbons,
stored in private drawers.
Though tolerant of others' mess
you keep your own space tidy,
work it attentively as edges
tighten with your body's stiffening.
But you will stretch
to its capacity, will not complain,
stifle all remindings of past vigour
that outstripped us all,
opened each day brightly
as we grew.

We look back, compare, regret internally;
you soldier on in your pragmatic school,
adapt, not mourn, keep dress and hair
meticulous, find an excuse
for cheerfulness in friends and busyness.
Just now and then a brittleness
speaks of a pain that each day
settles deeper in the shoulder, back,
shows us what it costs.
Your smile holds you up,
your strength, your management
of time; we will return it while the light
turns, hold it true and steady
in the balance of your brave dance.

'The Man on the Wall': a view from the other side

Response to a painting by L.S. Lowry, 1957.

It alarmed me when I glanced up from my path
beside the factory towards the church,
glanced up by chance and saw stretched out
full length on the wall a man, suspended
as it seemed in space above a plunging drop.
I shut my eyes and looked again
to verify, but there he was
outside the frame of usual or possible.

Down here I felt helpless, small,
while others passed me by, heads down
and heavy-footed, never looking up.
Was it only I who saw him there?
I wanted to call out, but no, too dangerous
to startle him and make him slip.
Had he reached a path he couldn't take,
were obstacles too large to overcome?
Was he balancing, precarious, between his life
and the unknown, sought the release
of nothingness, one foot on the edge?

But no, he was not balanced nervously,
nothing desperate about him there.
Indeed he looked quite calm, just like
a recumbent king or bishop in the church ahead.
At first I feared for him and then admired
his careless fortitude – the simple stepping off
the tracks, the lying down and staring up,
oblivious.

And all around me, people hurrying
with bowed heads, clumsy-footed,
dragging their bags, their little dogs,
seeing nothing but the ground,
while he stretches out above them
staring at the sky, shoes pointing up,
floating on the drift of his poised cigarette
away from rush and hurry
to another place.

Handstander

Buoyed on energy, upturned,
you spring into dilated space,
defy constraints.
You are circus artiste, wild child,
proud of your agility.
Upside down, your eyes graze grass,
your feet brush cloud.
You cycle with the sun, draw
new angles and perspectives
with the turning compass
of your legs.

Then you embrace another element
and slipping in the day's cool skin,
thread and spread your limbs
to water's flow, melt to fish and otter pelt,
borrow mayfly shimmer, catkin dust,
ride the current downstream,
pushing it back up to shore,
curl out and shake yourself.

You will not be grooved
on trammelled lines, sealed
in a synthetic, blinking box.
You can only sit so long, you stretch
the walls with your impatient mind,
spin imagination's coin
out onto the dazzle of the waiting sea,
the unmade road.

Troika!

Then, heat-flushed in the dancing room
we are swept to snow-steppes crisp
on the sledging track, bright in the moon's eye.
Violin bow quickens to a trotting pace
that turns our tired feet to prancing hooves
tripping a measure through the cycling spokes
of the circle set. We are spun
on a giddy ride, twisting and re-twisting
under arches, printing the grapevine,
then pushed:
Shute!
skirt and cloak flying, glowing cheek,
to the next sleigh on the wheel's arm,
off and round and round again
to collapse, breathless and laughing
at the journey's end as space of tundra
shrinks to wall, carillon of sleigh-bells fades,
snow melts to board beneath our feet.

The Voices

Now the great engine has ground down and stopped
and traffic noise has shrivelled to a hum
and died, other sounds are newly lifted
in the opened space and ring more brightly
in the emptiness.

There are the birds of course, which flute or sparkle
in a sky wiped clean, and human voices
thrown across the barrier of safety space
to houses opposite or echoing from shore
across the river's still.

The child in a pushed chair on the quiet street
speaks with eyes and limbs
to mother's voice and smiling face.
Percussive tributes to essential staff
ring out each week from doorsteps, balconies,
dogs adding trebles or a muffled bass.

Some voices rise to more uncertain pitch,
are edged with strain, anxiety.
For some, shut in and out,
the voices sound more loudly in the head
and multiply, untested on the air
in spreading silences, and waking
no reply.

We are held in a pause as on a lifted wave.
Sense peels to new acuity,
detects the movement of the sap, the blood.
The browsing mind picks up the footfall
of our days, the ticking heart,
and underneath, the wash and churn
of cycling themes in earth and sea
beyond the reach of voice or sight.

Balancing

'This morning's session will focus on balancing',
she announces from her tranquil space.
'We'll work within asymmetries
to find stability.'
That could be valuable; it's how we're living nowadays:
trying to keep our balance in a tightened place.
She keeps things calm; we wrap it round us gratefully
as we ease stiffness to mobility,
try to reconcile asymmetries.

We weigh the ache of things lost
against the richness of remembering,
or sudden joy against the jolt of memory -
the lift against the slip
of the heart.
We try to balance the sharpness of things
for the first time understood
against the misting at the edges of each day,
new quietness opening
beside the shrinking of the voice
and bustle of community,
try to hold a peace like water in cupped hands,
keep feet steady on uncertain paths.

We do breathing exercises from each lung
for evenness, are told to trust and loose the breath
to move the body with the mind,
sustain their health and equilibrium.

'It's not just about balancing on one leg',
she says, and of course it's more than that,
though at the moment
this is what we feel we're trying
and not quite managing
to do.

The Sea

Wild and dark the night sea
rearing on grey,
breaking on white
to flood the shore, withdraw
to leave its shining face,
the glisten of our melting steps.

Walkers moving steadily,
dog with lighted collar
skittering ahead, just visible.
We talk of floating things,
of challenges,
of how to find that core of calm,
headland flashing back
the lighthouse beam
to warn of twisting currents
in our passages.

We loop and return,
sand prints in our wake
dissolving to the prowling shapes
and yelps of foxes in the dunes,
squeal of ambushed prey,
thin bird calls from the rocks,
muffled bass of the sea's voice
breathing in the emptied space.

Helen Boyles - Biography

Helen Boyles is a writer and educator whose love of literature and the natural environment has shaped her career choices and recreational interests. She taught English language and literature for many years at Secondary and Further Education Level, and for the last 20 years has lectured in Humanities with the Open University. She has a Master's degree and PhD in 18th and early 19th-century English Literature, focusing in the latter on creative and religious 'enthusiasm' and their sometimes problematic relationship in writings from the Romantic era. This resulted in a book published by Routledge in 2017.

Currently she is exploring further the relationship between creativity and 'wild' walking in female writers from the same period. This chimes with her own love of long-distance walking, where nature and the reflection it inspires is a source of fulfilment on many levels. Helen has had two collections: *Catching Light (2016)* and *Transitions (2017)* published by *Indigo Dreams,* with poems also printed in journals and anthologies. During 2019 her work appeared in a collection of award-winning poems by the *Edward Thomas Fellowship;* and her piece on the burning of Notre Dame was translated into French and published in the January 2020 edition of Notre Dame's *Oecumenisme Informations.*

Helen is Co-Chair of the Devon-based Moor Poets, helping to promote and develop poetic talent in regular workshops based in and around Dartmoor. The Moor Poets are developing creative collaborations with local artists – a rewarding way of engaging with the environment and exploring its richness.

Palewell Press

Palewell Press is an independent publisher handling poetry, fiction and non-fiction with a focus on books that foster Justice, Equality and Sustainability. The Editor can be reached on enquiries@palewellpress.co.uk

www.ingramcontent.com/pod-product-compliance
Lightning Source LLC
Chambersburg PA
CBHW050507120526
44588CB00044B/1686